"Spiritual"

A BOOK OF
ORIGINAL POETRY

By:

D.B. Tyon, Rev.

TABLE OF CONTENTS

Chapter 4 – Short & Sweet (29)

*Forever Yours……………………….30
*Speak to My Heart……………. ...30
*Help me Heal…………………… ...31
*God Loves You…………………...31
*Which Way?……………………….32

Chapter 5 – Busy World (33)

*Remember Him…………………….34
*Take Time To Pray………………35-37
*Begin Again……………………….38
*Busy World……………………….39-44

CHAPTER 1

THE RIDE

THE RIDE

As I ride my stallion, to the mountain top -
reaching for the sky...
I find myself, lost in thought -
wondering how and why.

How did He do it, and why does He care?
And I ask Him that, when I get up there -
I dismount my horse - and I stop and stare...

For the beauty that surrounds me,
simply, just, *astounds* me -
all the sounds, around me -
every where.

I feel Him, deep within me...
Stirring something in me -
something, of which,
I am not *yet* aware.

I hear His Words, in the song of the birds;
and they fill the mountain air...
And the afternoon breeze,
as it blows through the trees,
is warning me - to beware.

He summons me, to notice,
the spider and bug...
And then, He gently gives me,
a warm, internal hug.
The spider, He says, is cunning and sly -
forever plotting, to trap the fly.

And many people, lay traps too -
hoping they will soon catch you.
So as you ride, on life's rough trail,
be sure to watch your gait...
For there are those, with tooth and nail -
who skillfully, lie, in wait.

And along the way, you will find,
those who like to be unkind...
Who laugh and tease,
those on their knees -
while *they*,
can't make up *their own* mind.

Then God tells me,
He won't leave me -
when all the others don't believe me -
and assures me, He will teach me,
right, from wrong.

He promises to guide me -
and to *always* stay beside me -
as the cricket's hum their slow, melodic song.

And as I descend the mountain,
passing by a fountain -
I feel *blessed* to be *alive*...
upon the earth.
And I *thank* God, for all His gifts to me -
and tell Him to do as He wishes, with me -
for *I was* His servant, *already*...
at my birth.

I like to think, He understands...
What He always meant to me -
but I wanted to do, what I wanted to do -
and to be, what I wanted to be.

And so, in my youth, I strayed a bit,
from that straight and narrow path...
But I like to think, He understood -
and maybe, even laughed.

And through the years,
as I grew older...
His hold on me - well, it grew bolder.
And though I resisted, to some extent,
I never fought too hard -
because, after all, it is God's game;
and He holds the ultimate card.

And as I remember, those wonderful days...
My life has changed, in so many ways -
before, I was strong,
and now, I am weak...
It didn't take long,
to turn me humble and meek.

I can no longer get upon my horse -
for gravity is a mighty force.
With broken leg, I sit and write -
to tell this tale to you...
Somewhat prepared, but still, not quite -
for what it is, I must do.

My ride, is not yet over...
Onward, I go, still -
on an endless search,
for the perfect church -
climbing, up life's hill.
The Mormon Church, disappointed me...
The Universal Life Church has anointed me.
But I feel, that God *ordained* me, long ago.

The Church just never *knew me* -
they said, God *wouldn't,* talk *to* me...
But how in the world, does *anybody know?*

**I know God, as well as *any* man -
as well, as any human can.**

He walks with me,
and I with Him...
(when I can keep that pace).
And I will *always* be...
whether *beside*, or behind,
On *His* team - while I'm riding life's race.

So, though I may not *belong*,
to a church -
right or wrong...
I *long*, to belong to Him.

And whenever I ask,
"Lord, show me my task..."
He answers, with vigor and vim.

And He tells me to write,
both day and night -
He *tells me* write... about **Him.**

And now that I know, the bulk of His plan -
I will watch where I go, and do what I can...
And though I am scared, of crowds, just a bit -
I'm not scared of *any man.*
For God is with me - this is it -
I can do it...
I know that I can.

Then He fills me with words,
about life and death...
He sharpens my senses,
and halts my breath -
but only, for a moment or two.
And with my hands shaking,
at the task I am facing,
He tells me, again...
what to do.

He says to reach out, to those who are lost;
Who would sell their soul, at any cost -
to the young and confused...
and the scared - and the tossed.
To tell them, they control *their own* life's ride -
we can live with *humility,* or live with pride.

Our body is ours -
to do with, as we please;
as we *traverse* this physical plain.

With doors to open,
and doors to close;
there's so much to lose...
yet, so much to gain.

So walk through any door you want...
Some will help you - others, will taunt.

And if you get stuck,
or lose your way -
all you have to do...
Is take the time to stop and pray -
and God will rescue you.

Yes, I like to remember,
those rides in September...
As the leaves crunched beneath my steed.

And when I recall,
those days in the Fall...
I thank God, for planting that seed.
Enjoy the ride.
***

CHAPTER 2

PERSONAL

Who Am I?

As I pass the mirror,
I stop and stare -
who *is* that person, standing there?
I hardly know her anymore,
that person, who I was before.

She looks at me,
with those trusting eyes -
and a soul that's seven times her size.
And the more I look,
the more she changes...
The figure, before me - it rearranges.
She stretches and turns,
as for wisdom, she yearns -
And all at once, I realize...

It is me, that I see -
looking back nervously...
And regardless, what the mirror shows,
This soul that I feel -
that's what is real...
Not what this body knows.

I am, who I am...
For God made me, she.
I am her.
She is me.
We are one - me and she.
And I believe I am who *God* wants me to be.

So, inside-out, I will walk,
through this world on my own...
Small and scared -
tired and timid -
but *not* ever *really* alone.

With my soul exposed,
I wear this shell...
As I walk through life -
and go, *through* Hell.
And the girl that I was,
I always will be...
Even though, it's not her, now -
I see looking at me.

In a body that's aging, withered and worn -
with clothing, now baggy, tattered and torn...
I pour out my soul,
so that other's might learn -
that they, too, should teach -
when it comes to their turn.

And no matter what image,
the mirror might see,
I trust, in this one thing...
That *I am*, exactly,
where *He* wants me to be;
and through all this, my soul, He will bring.

***

<u>Crazy?</u>

I love it, when I hear from God...
as oft times, I *know I do.*
Some people really think I'm odd,
but others hear Him, too...

How do I hear Him,
you might want to know?
He speaks to me,
every where I go.

In the afternoon breeze,
or a morning rain -
He speaks to me,
in the *back of my brain.*

He speaks to my heart,
and makes it race -
and, sometimes, He speaks to me,
face to face.

You say, that sounds crazy?
I once thought so, too.
But give Him a chance...
He'll get *hold* of you!
***

<u>Where is My Mind?</u>

As I sit here tonight and rethink the day,
there were so many things, I wanted to say...
Of course, I can't remember ten minutes ago -
so how in the world, will I ever know...
The thoughts that came earlier -
just hours ago?
They leave a curious gnawing,
and a humbled ego.

Sometimes I wonder, why my mind leaves me...
And then I worry that no one believes me.
I'm young - it's true - but I'm a mother too...
And that, in itself, can age you.

Four children, I've born -
and kissed every morn'
and years, I have watched, roll away.
I married too young...
Never could hold my tongue -
and asked God for strength every day.

And when my mind fails me,
and this body ails me...
I just have to remember to pray.
Then God reassures me -
comforts and lures me -
to play the game, His way.

He tells me, He will sustain me,
and strengthen my body again...

And He will *not* restrain me,
from straying, a bit, now and then.
But then, in the same breath,
I hear Him ask me -
to try harder every day...
To keep *Him*, on my mind,
and my troubles behind -
and to watch the things I say.

For we are living in a dreadful age -
when God is thought of, less and less...
And before we turn another page,
we must caution, persuade and press.
I am frightened, for mankind,
so *there are some* things that I must stress...
For, if *we all,* lose sight of Him,
the world will be a mess.

I'm afraid, my friend,
it's just a matter of time,
before the light, goes dim...
So help me, to remind the world,
where we would be without Him -
if not for the love God has for us,
even when we forget to pray...
So have faith - be cheerful;
and never fearful...
God will find a way.

***

It's all about Him

God is in control...
Yet we are in control -
every day it's us...

But evermore, it's Him.

He speaks to us each day...
Yet we go on our way –
looking at ourselves -
filling up our shelves...

And forgetting about Him.

Sometimes I feel so lost...
Yet He paid such a cost -
to give this gift to us...

I can never forget about Him.

He knows that I am weak...
That I'm afraid to speak -
yet still, he trusts in me...

So I must tell about Him.

I don't want to be thought deranged...
But it all seems to be so arranged –
the way that life began...
It's all just one big plan –

and it's all because of Him.

It scares me to be known...
I feel naked and alone -
speaking out loud -
in front of a crowd...

So I just want to write about Him.

More and more He urges me...
Every year, the more I see -
that it's my duty - my debt to pay...

To tell the world about Him.
***

My Life is Yours

My life is in Your hands...
But no one understands;
they think I've lost my mind...
why are they so unkind?

I once gave my life to You...
saying, "do as You wish to do" -
and You have led me Here...
A far, far cry, from *There*.

But my friends and family,
they wonder, about me.
My grandma says she prays,
that I will find my way...

Back to the church I left -
but *they* don't want my Gift...
Women *cannot* preach -
that is what *They teach* !

But Lord, *I always* **knew You**,
deep within my heart...
And knew my strength was through You -
I was Yours, right from the start.
***

<u>Lord Help Me</u>

Lord, please tell me, how I know…

If it is or isn't so

that You were Jesus,

and Jesus, You -

anymore than we are, too.

I've always felt You in my heart,

and always felt like such a part

of a world where *once* I did belong…

But the one I lived in felt so wrong.

People talk and people preach -

but no one knows just what to teach.

They say they do,

when they really don't…

They promise to do things,

they really won't.

People lie and cheat and steal -

and then they tell you what to feel,

what to think and how to live...

Few remember how to give.

Fewer less, remember You,

unless they sit in their church pew.

They spout righteousness,

despite their sins -

and go back home to sin again -

never giving a second thought,

to Your presence,

as their follies are wrought.

Help me Lord, to know what to do...

And help me, I pray, to teach what is true.

***

CHAPTER 3

THE BEAUTY OF NATURE

The Power of God's Flower

As I look upon a flower,
I can't help but notice how...
It harnesses so much power,
in the *here and now* –

It's beauty is enchanting;
a mesmerizing view...
You will find it quite entrancing -
that bright and brilliant hue.

And if you look, closely enough,
you'll see the face of God -
Pure and good - delicate, yet tough...
And the stem, *His* mighty rod.

A flower represents God's grace, and fertility...
Grace, He gives us, when we fall -
if we ask with humility.

And with each passing day,
we have a chance to redeem -
our children, our souls, and our nation...

But time passes away...
And somehow, it seems -
We, are the lost generation.

When we look at a flower -
and don't acknowledge God's power,
it's, to Him, as a slap in the face.

Because the earth, that's beneath us,
was given... *bequeathed,* to us,
for the sole purpose of running this race.

Still, the choice to run, is yours to make,
some people choose to walk -
and some people choose to close their eyes...
And speak with lofty talk.

"God is dead," some people say -
But God is far from dead...
He's with us, in the air we breathe -
and deep inside our head.

He left clear signs of our evolution,
planted seeds of doubt in our heart...
And told us stories, without solution -
to encourage us to start.

A long, long journey, mankind has made -
through flood and famine and violence laid...
Laid upon our head.

Tests we have taken -
and we've been mistaken...
But always, we've been fed.

And as a whole, if we hold strong -
pray night and day - our whole life long...
I have heard it said,
that in the end, *not one,* will be dead.

So cling tightly to your faith, my friend...
no matter what you do.
Whatever life will bring our way,
God *will* see us through.

Even those, who do not know it...
God will help to see -
He takes His time, sometimes, to show it;
but, eventually...

He'll hold out His hand,
and you'll understand –
If your eyes are open,
and your heart is willing...

how the power, of God's flower,
is so thrilling.
***

Nature's Musicians

The music of nature, fills the air...
Chirping crickets, every where -
birds that sing and leaves that whistle;
grass blades rub, across the thistle.

The locust buzz is shrill and deep,
and lulls me to a peaceful sleep.
Where, in my dreams, I hear it, still...
On it goes, and on, until...

The musicians, one by one, sleep too -
but there's still much more for them to do.
Tomorrow is another day,
and once again, they will play.

* * *

Spring Grass

How is it, that the grass does grow,
after it's Winter sleep?
I'll tell you how - because I know,
by the company that I keep.

His power is strong,
and though Winter is long...

By His warmth and His light,
the grass comes back to life -
as if wakened by a sweet song of birth.

His energy soars,
deep into it's pores -
and it gently springs forth, from the earth.

It drinks of the dew -
and rises anew-

just as Jesus rose, that Spring...
And it gets stronger each day -
in every way -
as it listens, to birds, while they sing.

***

CHAPTER 4

SHORT & SWEET

Forever Yours

Lord, I am forever Yours...
Please help me find my way.

Life's hallway, holds so many doors...
Forgive me, when I stray.

Forever, I will love You...
Forever, I will praise –

Your Son, Your Name...
One and the same.

Humbly Yours,
'till the end of days.
***

Speak to My Heart

Speak to my heart, Lord - loud and clear;
Speak to my heart, that I may hear...
To hear you, Lord, is all I want -
every night and day;
to hear you, Lord, without a doubt -
knowing what you say.
* * *

Help Me Heal

Lord, thank you, for another day...
Please forgive me, when I forget to pray –

Your love, I feel...
Will help me heal –

and Your light, will show the way.
***

God Loves You

No matter what you do,

God loves you...

He shows it everyday.

He wakes your soul,

and keeps you whole -

and takes your pain away.

***

Which Way?

Under, over - down or up...

which way should I go?

Left or right - or right or left -

I really do not know.

If I just go straight ahead,

how can I go wrong?

I=ll let God lead me,

protect and feed me...

and fill my heart with song.

***

CHAPTER 5

BUSY WORLD

<u>Remember Him</u>

Alone, I sit, but not alone;
in my bed at night.
We talk for hours, without a phone...
Sometimes, til morning light.

The conversation is quiet,
there's no need for verbal speech.
Everyone should try it -
for God has much to teach.

But He can only reach you,
when you reach out to Him...
And if you let Him teach you,
your life won't seem so dim.

He is always with us -
always very near...
And anything you wish to discuss,
He's always glad to hear.

It's not that hard to talk to God...
He knows your every thought.
You really shouldn't think it odd,
to speak out loud, or not.

For, as long as He is on your mind,
He is connected to you...
You'll feel Him beside, in front and behind,
Just remember Him, in ALL that you do.

***

Take Time to Pray

Do you ever feel the need to pray,
but hurry on along your way...
All the while, to your self, you say,
"I'll pray, later on, today."

But, nighttime comes,
as it always does...
And everything is,
as it always was.

And exhausted, from your day of labor -
and worrying about, your bills
and your neighbor -
what things you have,
and what things you don't,
what you'll get to do and what you won't...

You drop on your bed,
all clean and fed -
and forget, that your prayers,
yet *haven't* been said.

But, there comes a day of reckoning -
when we must answer, to God's beckoning.
And eventually,
you'll bow your knee -
and see, that He is wise.
For He has a way,
each and every day -
of opening someone's eyes.

Verily, there comes a season,
when, without rhyme or reason...
On a night, dark and still -
you'll *realize,* God's Will...
As it hits you -
He is here!

So, you bow your head,
and humbly say,
"Lord, I thank you, for today.

Please help me through tomorrow...
and each day after, that I borrow -
until I come, to see you again...
I understand, I *can't know,* when.

Stay close beside me -
protect me and guide me -
and help me to stay strong.
Influence my choices...
Teach me your voices -
and fill my heart, with song.

You fill my days,
in so many ways...
With small reminders of You.
The warm sun's rays. -
And the cool evening haze...
And the satiny morning dew.

So Lord, forgive me when I stumble...
Do your best, to keep me humble.
But know, that when I stumble, it's because...

You were gracious enough -
though, your lessons are tough -
to free me, from your laws."

And as you finish the prayer of a sinner,
the width of your worries
becomes much thinner -
Then your tired eyes will close,
as, your weary heart then slows...

And you surrender yourself to slumber.
Then by God's great power,
in that mystic hour...
You'll dream, magical dreams,
without number.

He'll speak to you,
in your dreams that night -
at least, He will...
if you ask Him right.

I, like you, have fought my whole life long...
Sometimes, I feel weak,
when I desire to feel strong.

But I've learned, my weakness goes away -
when I remember,
to take time, to stop and pray.
***

BEGIN AGAIN

There comes a time in all our lives,
when hopelessness sets in;
when all seems lost and we find we ought,
begin our lives again.

We must rise up when we are down,
in order to stand and fight;
for in the darkest night, you will find,
it's easiest to see the light.

No matter where life leads us
In good times and in bad,
the love of God still feeds us...
whether happy love, or sad.

Through the best times He has talked to me,
as I went through my day;
and in the worst times, He's walked with me,
though *I've* felt far away.

I thank the Lord, for this life I lead,
though far from Him, I stray;
Still He stays with me, through adversity,
and comforts me, day by day.

***

BUSY WORLD

Things to do... places to be.
Things to take care of and people to see.
Busy you, busy me...
Imagine where the world would be,
without Him to guide our spirit -
a voice of Wisdom - if you can hear it.

Running here, and running there...
Always running, everywhere.
On the go - in a hurry to die -
never really knowing why.

We push ahead,
on our life's journey...
Though the path is rocky
and sometimes thorny –

and we forge our way,

through good times and bad -

for the most part, being thankful,

for the good times we've had.

But we don't understand,

the one thing we should...

that the *bad times* are what teach us,

more than the good.

We should be most thankful

for those difficult days -

for they have helped us in many ways.

Durations of despair,

lasting any length...

It is those times that build spiritual strength.

Most of us don't notice –

as we crawl in our hole -

but what we do, *on days of sadness*,

is *look* into our soul.

Whether you are aware, or not...

You maintain a special spot.

God is present in your life,

as much as you allow -

But regardless of acceptance,

He loves you anyhow.

This life is just an experience...

to teach us right from wrong.

It's His way of building our character –

letting us struggle, our whole life long.

But His world is always waiting...

The pains of this world, abating -

While constantly, we struggle and worry...

Why are we in such a hurry?

Life is too short to be callous and cold -
before we all know it, we will be old.

And the thing that God hopes,
that we will all learn,
as we go through this life –
and suffer and yearn –

is that, the very most important part,
comes from matters of the heart...

It's that we love,
that we nurture...
That we learn to care.
It is simply to know that He is there.

The first lesson in life,
as a babe, in warm arms,
*we learn **that** kind person*
will keep us from harm.

And the one thing that's certain...

The one thing we know...

is that, **that** love will *always be there.*

And the love that they give us –

it helps us to grow -

and it shapes us in ways

we couldn't possibly know.

God's love, does the same,

in a spiritual way -

"Intuition" or "instinct"...

"gut feelings," you say?

That is God... urging you, every day –

to do what is right - to do what is good.

Imploring you always, to do what you should.

Though God's arms are not flesh...

they are a safe mesh -

to keep us from falling too far.

Throughout your life... in melee and strife,

He watches over you, wherever you are.

Opportunities, He presents,

when needs arise -

and discipline, He provides,

to make us wise.

In this busy world,

as we go through each day -

hurrying, worrying,

and pushing Him away –

He loves us, regardless...

of what we do, or don't, say.

But we *should* try to thank Him,

once in a while, anyway.

***

www.ingramcontent.com/pod-product-compliance
Lightning Source LLC
Chambersburg PA
CBHW031635040426
42452CB00007B/839